# LET'S PLAY SPORTS!

# Lacrosse

by Kieran Downs

BELLWETHER MEDIA • MINNEAPOLIS, MN

**Blastoff! Readers** are carefully developed by literacy experts to build reading stamina and move students toward fluency by combining standards-based content with developmentally appropriate text.

**Level 1** provides the most support through repetition of high-frequency words, light text, predictable sentence patterns, and strong visual support.

**Level 2** offers early readers a bit more challenge through varied sentences, increased text load, and text-supportive special features.

**Level 3** advances early-fluent readers toward fluency through increased text load, less reliance on photos, advancing concepts, longer sentences, and more complex special features.

★ **Blastoff! Universe**

**Reading Level**

**Grade K**

**Grades 1–3**

**Grade 4**

This edition first published in 2021 by Bellwether Media, Inc.

No part of this publication may be reproduced in whole or in part without written permission of the publisher. For information regarding permission, write to Bellwether Media, Inc., Attention: Permissions Department, 6012 Blue Circle Drive, Minnetonka, MN 55343.

Library of Congress Cataloging-in-Publication Data

Names: Downs, Kieran, author.
Title: Lacrosse / by Kieran Downs.
Description: Minneapolis, MN : Bellwether Media, 2021. | Series: Blastoff! readers. Let's play sports! | Includes bibliographical references and index. | Audience: Ages 5-8 | Audience: Grades K-1 | Summary: "Relevant images match informative text in this introduction to lacrosse. Intended for students in kindergarten through third grade"– Provided by publisher.
Identifiers: LCCN 2020029219 (print) | LCCN 2020029220 (ebook) | ISBN 9781644874264 (library binding) | ISBN 9781648341038 (ebook)
Subjects: LCSH: Lacrosse–Juvenile literature.
Classification: LCC GV989.14 .D69 2021 (print) | LCC GV989.14 (ebook) | DDC 796.36/2–dc23
LC record available at https://lccn.loc.gov/2020029219
LC ebook record available at https://lccn.loc.gov/2020029220

Editor: Rebecca Sabelko     Designer: Josh Brink

Printed in the United States of America, North Mankato, MN.

# Table of Contents

# What Is Lacrosse?

Lacrosse is a team sport played on a field.

Players try to score **goals**. The team that scores the most goals in 60 minutes wins!

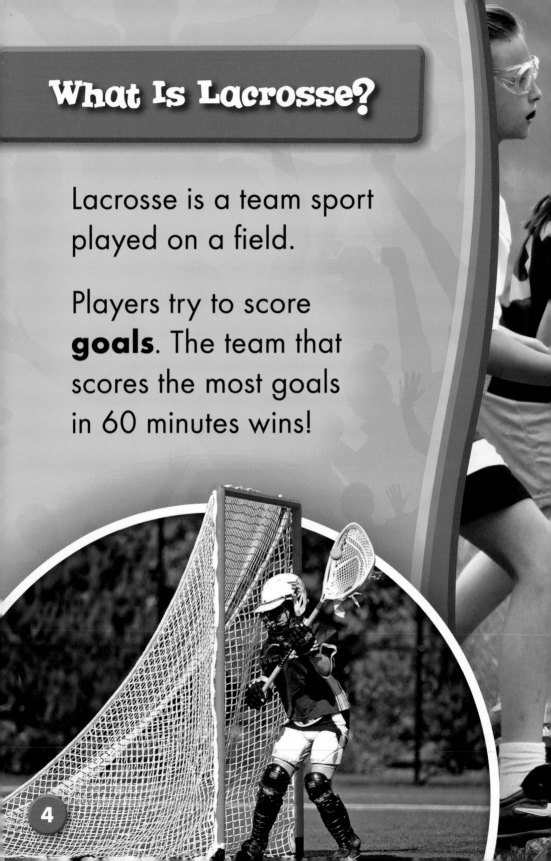

Lacrosse was invented by the **Six Nations of the Iroquois**. The sport dates back hundreds of years!

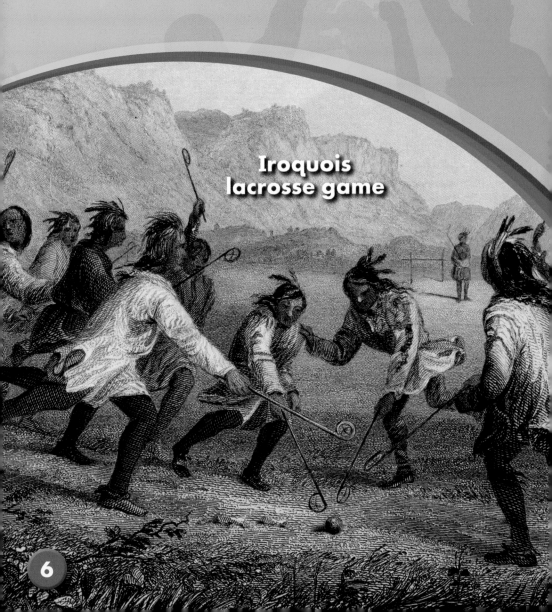

Iroquois lacrosse game

# PAUL RABIL

- Midfielder
- Major League Lacrosse (MLL), National Lacrosse League (NLL), Premier Lacrosse League (PLL)
- Accomplishments:
  - MLL All-Star 10 times
  - MLL MVP 2 times
  - Co-founder of the Premier Lacrosse League

Today, it is most popular in the United States.

# What Are the Rules for Lacrosse?

cross

Lacrosse teams have 10 or 12 players. Players use a **cross** to throw the ball into a net.

Nets have **creases** around them. Players must throw from outside the crease.

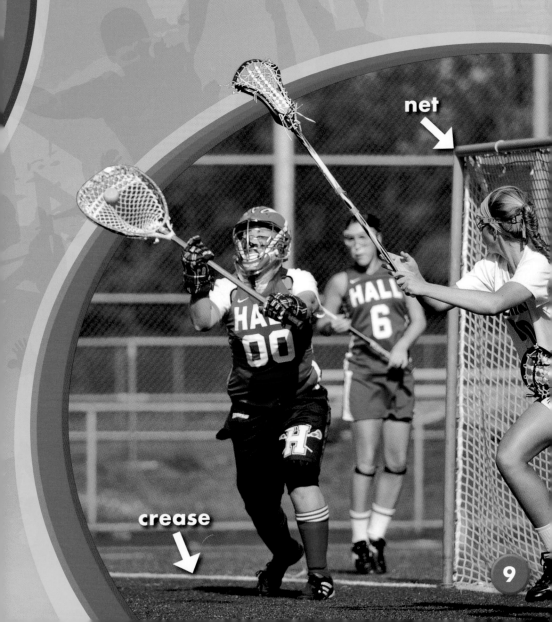

net

crease

Games start with a **face-off**. One **attacker** from each team goes to the **midfield line**.

face-off

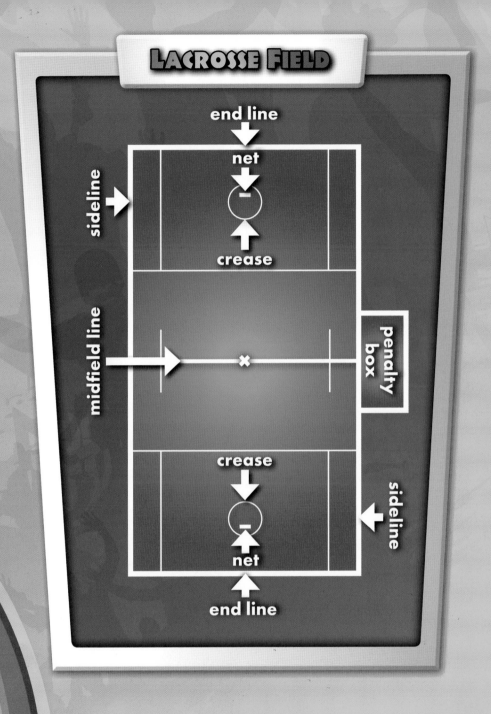

# LACROSSE FIELD

end line

net

crease

sideline

midfield line

penalty box

crease

sideline

net

end line

They battle for the ball!

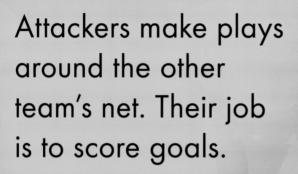

Attackers make plays around the other team's net. Their job is to score goals.

**Defenders** try to stop attackers from scoring.

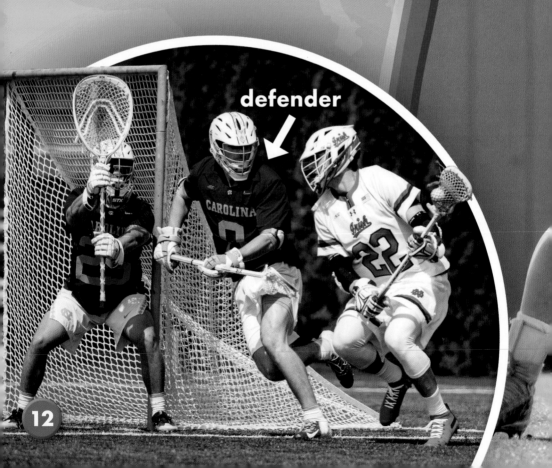

defender

attacker

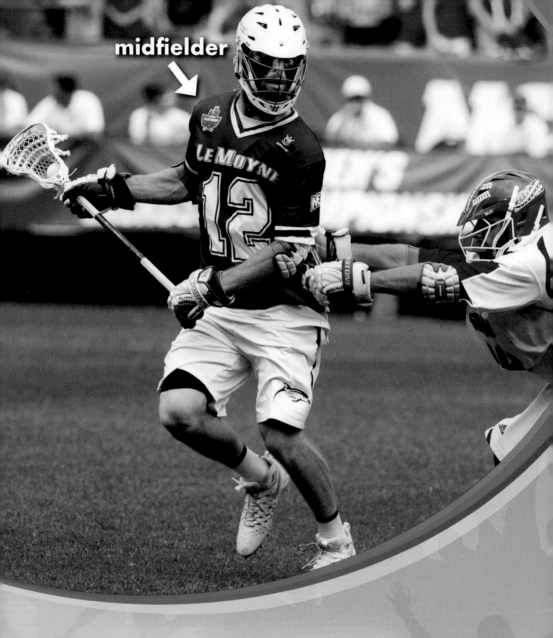

midfielder

**Midfielders** play both **offense** and defense. They pass the ball up the field.

They also help
attackers score.

Sometimes players break rules. They are sent to the **penalty box**.

penalty

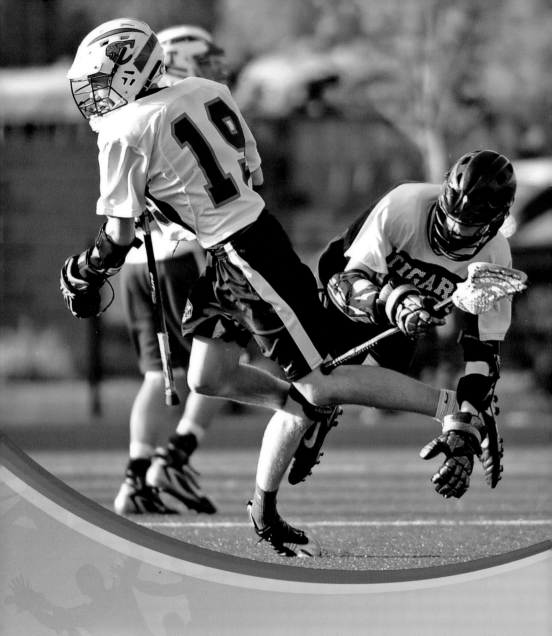

They cannot play for up to three minutes. Their team must play with one less player.

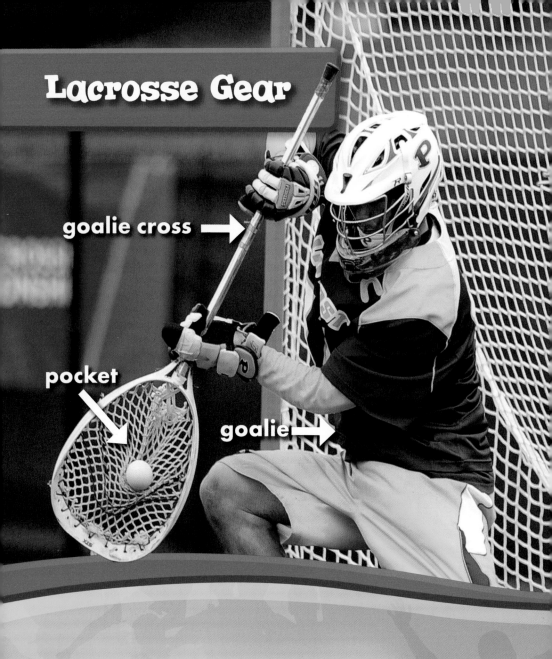

# Lacrosse Gear

goalie cross →

pocket ↓

goalie →

Crosses have a pocket
on one end. This lets players
catch and throw the ball.

## Lacrosse Gear

helmet

cross

gloves

ball

**Goalies** use special crosses with bigger pockets.

Players wear a lot of safety gear. Gloves protect their hands. Helmets keep their heads safe.

They are ready to play. Go team!

# Glossary

**attacker**—a player who tries to score goals; attackers can only play in offensive areas.

**creases**—circular lines around the nets; players must throw the ball outside the crease to score a goal.

**cross**—a lacrosse stick

**defenders**—players who try to stop the other team from scoring; defenders must play on the defensive half of the field, near their own net.

**face-off**—a way to begin play in which two players try to get the ball

**goalies**—players who guard the goal to keep the other team from scoring

**goals**—points scored when the ball goes into the lacrosse net

**midfield line**—the line that marks the middle of a lacrosse field

**midfielders**—players who move the ball from defenders to attackers; midfielders can go anywhere on the field.

**offense**—the team that has the ball and is trying to score

**penalty box**—the area beside the field where a player who has broken a rule sits for a certain amount of time

**Six Nations of the Iroquois**—a group of Native Americans that includes the Mohawk, Oneida, Onondaga, Cayuga, Seneca, and Tuscarora nations

# To Learn More

**AT THE LIBRARY**

Kingsley, Imogen. *Boys' Lacrosse Fun*. North Mankato, Minn.: Capstone, 2020.

Kingsley, Imogen. *Girls' Lacrosse Fun*. North Mankato, Minn.: Capstone, 2020.

Sports Illustrated Kids. *My First Book of Lacrosse: A Rookie Book*. New York, N.Y.: Time Inc. Books, 2018.

**ON THE WEB**

Factsurfer.com gives you a safe, fun way to find more information.

1. Go to www.factsurfer.com.

2. Enter "lacrosse" into the search box and click 🔍.

3. Select your book cover to see a list of related content.

# Index